Norwich over the Water: walk 2

Start at St Andrew's Hall and walk along St George's Street, crossing the River Wensum at St George's (Blackfriars) Bridge to **Norwich** **over the Water (page 23).** Turn right along **Colegate (pages 24–25)** and right, at the end, across Fye Bridge to Wensum Street. Cross the street and walk up Elm Hill to take you back to St Andrew's Hall.

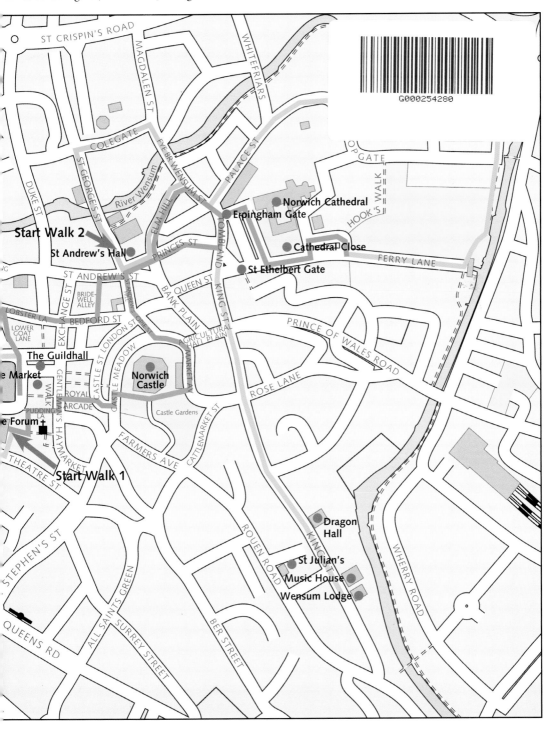

There was once a saying in Norwich that people could visit a different pub each day of the year and worship at a different church each week. The Normans built not only the great cathedral here, but also more than 50 parish churches. Thirty-one of these wonderful medieval churches still stand. Although only nine are used for regular worship, their ancient stonework, imposing towers and peaceful gardens add to the atmosphere of a city whose main streets are still laid out in their medieval pattern. There are also plenty of modern attractions – excellent shopping, theatres, galleries, riverside walks, cafés, restaurants and pubs. Much of the centre of the city is traffic-free, so visitors may fully enjoy the interweaving of historic beauty and 21st-century pleasures.

A short history

Norowic was one of the many Anglo-Saxon settlements along the banks of the River Wensum in marshy East Anglia. Gradually the disparate communities merged to become one large, walled town. By the time the Normans arrived in 1066, Norwich was already an important centre, with its own mint and profitable trade by river and sea with other parts of England, Scandinavia, Russia, the Low Countries and the Rhineland. The Normans built the cathedral and castle, established new trading patterns and welcomed city status in 1194.

Of all the thriving trades, weaving became the most important and profitable. A large class of wealthy merchants and traders, who ran the city, evolved. Norwich was the centre for making worsted cloth (named after the nearby village where it originated), for which there was huge demand. Periods of disruption occurred, including the Peasants' Revolt of the late 14th century and, later in 1549, Robert Kett led an army of 20,000 agricultural workers and small farmers that took the city in protest at increased rents and the removal of grazing rights on common land. There was massive destruction before the rebels were suppressed and Kett was hanged at Norwich Castle. Then came a decline in the worsted industry, but that was solved in 1565 by the importation of 'strangers' – families of expert cloth workers from the Netherlands, who brought different techniques to breathe new life into the trade. They also brought their canaries with them, which explains the city's long association with the colourful little bird.

Prosperous years followed and new banking, insurance and brewing businesses sprang up in the 18th century. Grand buildings such as the Assembly House and the Theatre Royal were established, while many private houses received a Georgian facelift. The first half of the 20th century saw a splendid new City Hall built to replace the historic Guildhall which was no longer large enough, while the futuristic Forum, dominating the marketplace, heralds a bright new millennium for Norwich.

In 2012 Norwich was named England's first UNESCO City of Literature in recognition of its literary past, contemporary strengths and future potential with regards to literature, creative writing, reading and the literary arts. The city joins the likes of Edinburgh, Melbourne, Iowa City, Dublin and Reykjavik.

The Forum

The Forum with the Church of St Peter Mancroft on the right

The great soaring glass and steel outline of the horseshoe-shaped Forum, standing above Market Place, is a magnet to visitors. This innovative centre, opened in 2001, is home to one of the most modern libraries in the country; the Norfolk and Norwich Millennium Library; the Fusion Digital Gallery; touring shows and exhibitions; the tourist information centre; a café-bar and restaurant; and regional BBC television and radio stations. A variety of events takes place in the area outside, including the monthly Norfolk Diet Farmers' Market.

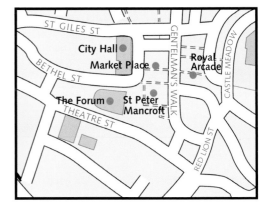

The City Hall

Two magnificent Abyssinian lions guard the entrance to this award-winning art-deco building opened in 1938. The painted ceiling above the stairs shows badgers, ducks and other Norfolk wildlife.

City Hall lion

Fusion Digital Gallery

The Fusion screen is free and is open every day except Sundays and Bank Holidays. It shows a variety of digital screenings and plays on a loop, so it doesn't matter if you miss the start.

The Church of St Peter Mancroft

This, the grandest of Norwich's many churches, built between 1430 and 1455, is sometimes mistaken for the cathedral. There was no St Peter Mancroft – the original dedication was to the saints Peter and Paul. You can see symbols of both saints by the north porch door. As the Norman market became established in the 'Magna Crofta' or 'Great Meadow' just below the church, the name became shortened to reflect its location. The great east window contains a treasury of medieval painted glass, much of it made by immigrant Flemish craftsmen.

Pudding Lane and Market Place

Narrow Pudding Lane alongside St Peter Mancroft is where the cloth merchants once had their shops. Steps lead down into the colourful Market Place, which has been home to traders for more than 900 years – since they decamped from their stalls at Tombland (see page 8).

Gentleman's Walk and the Royal Arcade

This open promenade below the crowded market was once lined with comfortable coaching inns. Look for the entrance to the shop-lined Royal Arcade, incorporating the grand façade of the Royal Hotel. This art nouveau fantasy, designed by George Skipper, was opened in 1899. A peacock frieze and soft green and grey-blue tiles adorn the walls, while ornate lamps hang from the glass ceiling. Exit beneath a

The Royal Arcade

glass screen decorated with white doves and green leaves. Ahead you'll see the great keep of Norwich Castle.

Hot stuff

It has been 200 years since Jeremiah Colman first started making mustard in Norwich. Find out more at Colman's Mustard Shop and Museum in the Royal Arcade.

Market Place

Norwich Castle

The Normans came to Norwich soon after their conquest of England in 1066. The city was then one of the most important boroughs in the country, rich and powerful enough to have its own mint. In 1067 they constructed a steep hill here, on top of which they built a wooden castle for their kings. Just 60 years later the wooden building was replaced by the stone keep of the castle you see today. In 1345 the building became the county gaol; public executions were carried out at the castle until 1867.

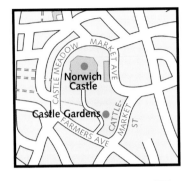

Norwich Castle Museum and Art Gallery

A Victorian restoration saw the end of the gaol and the opening of the castle as a museum and art gallery. Now it holds several outstanding collections of art, natural history, archaeology and historical artefacts.

The Keep

This is the heart of the castle, the original entrance with elaborately carved stonework. You can walk around the upper gallery or see the five garderobes – the four-berth lavatories that line one wall. There are many treasures displayed in the keep, including 'Snap' the brightly painted wooden dragon who traditionally plagued onlookers during the annual St George's Day processions.

Norwich Castle   *Castle Museum*

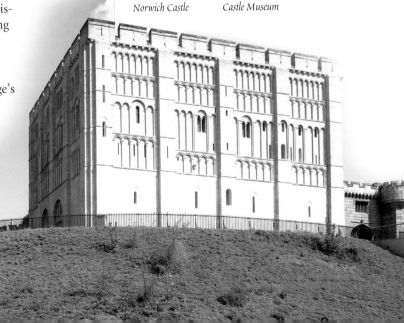

Norwich School of Art collections

The two great masters of this regional school of painting in early 19th-century Norwich were John Sell Cotman and John Crome. Much of their work can be seen in the galleries at the castle.

Castle Gardens and Green

The original wide ditch surrounding the castle became public gardens in 1849. Castle Green, with views over the city and a children's play area, is built above the Castle Mall shopping complex and lies next to the castle.

Love among the butterflies

Margaret Fountaine was a well-brought-up Victorian girl until a sad love affair set her off on a lifetime's journey hunting butterflies and men in Europe and further afield. The Fountaine-Neimy butterfly collection in the museum achieved great popularity when her two frank books *Love Among the Butterflies* and *Butterflies and Late Loves* were published 40 years after her death in 1940.

Castle Gardens

Set in stone

As you walk towards the castle you'll notice beautifully engraved stone panels set in the curving wall. Follow the eleven carvings to the castle door. Each carving reflects something in the museum collection, while the lines of verse are from different writers.

Royal Norfolk Regimental Museum

Royal Norfolk Regimental Museum

This museum can be visited at Norwich Castle. It charts the history of the Royal Norfolk Regiment and its collections include army uniform, kit, personal letters and diaries. Also on offer is an interactive timeline so visitors can take a digital journey through the Regiment's history.

7

St Andrew's Hill

As you cross into Opie Street you're confronted with narrow streets full of interesting shops and beautiful old buildings. Cross London Street into St Andrew's Hill, where, halfway down on the left, is the fine flintwork of the wall of The Museum of Norwich at The Bridewell (see page 19), once a grand house, built in 1370.

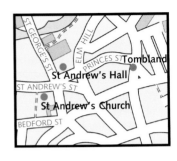

St Andrew's Hall

St Andrew's Church & St Andrew's Hall

St Andrew's Church contains a chapel and monuments to the Sucklings, prominent 16th-century citizens. Opposite is The Halls, formerly a church belonging to the Black Friars, now used for concerts and craft and antiques fairs. It is one of the 22 surviving medieval churches and their green spaces that are no longer used for regular worship.

Tombland

When the Normans arrived here in Norwich in the late 11th century, they found a prosperous settlement run by Anglo-Saxons and Danes, themselves earlier invaders. The heart of the borough was 'Tum Land', meaning a large open space. Here was the market and the centre of administration, until the Normans moved the market to the area where it still stands – not far from their new castle – as they cleared Tombland to make way for the cathedral in 1096. Today, Tombland is a spacious meeting place in the heart of Norwich Cathedral Quarter outside the cathedral close, its tree-lined pavements full of restaurants, cafés and small shops.

Tombland

London Street

Cathedral gates

Two magnificent gates guard the cathedral close. The larger St Ethelbert's Gate to the right allows entry to both pedestrians and vehicles while the Erpingham Gate leads directly to the cathedral's main entrance.

Carnary Chapel
Erpingham Gate
Norwich Cathedral
TOMBLAND
UPPER CLOSE
LOWER CL
QUEEN ST
St Ethelbert's Gate

St Ethelbert's Gate

This gate is named after St Ethelbert, the young king of East Anglia murdered in AD 794. St George is shown over the arch fighting the dragon (see page 15).

Erpingham Gate

This richly decorated gate was given in 1420 by Sir Thomas Erpingham, who led the English archers to victory at the Battle of Agincourt. His effigy kneels in prayer above the archway.

Edith Cavell

Just outside the Erpingham Gate is the memorial bust to Edith Cavell, the daughter of a Norfolk vicar. Edith, a nurse during the First World War, was executed in 1915 by the Germans for helping British and French prisoners escape from Belgium. 'Patriotism is not enough; I must have no hatred or bitterness towards anyone,' she wrote the night before she was shot. Her grave lies in Life's Green near the cathedral's east end.

Edith Cavell

Erpingham Gate

Carnary Chapel

Just inside the Erpingham Gate is the chapel of Norwich School. This was built over an old charnel house, where bones were stored.

Local hero

An impressive statue of Admiral Lord Nelson dominates the grassy area of the Upper Close. The Norfolk-born sea-going hero was, for a short while, a pupil at Norwich School, now an independent school, set in the cathedral close.

Norwich Cathedral

A great sense of space impresses visitors stepping through the west door of the Cathedral Priory of the Holy and Undivided Trinity. Built as a penance by Norwich's first bishop, Herbert de Losinga, who combined the great church with a bishop's palace and a Benedictine monastery, the cathedral was begun in 1096 and completed just 50 years later. It was built of local flint and limestone from Caen in Normandy.

The nave

The comparative narrowness of the nave increases the feeling of the tremendous height of its vaulted roof. In 1463 the original wooden roof was destroyed by fire and replaced by stone vaulting, whose rib-joints or bosses tell the Bible story from the Creation in Genesis to Revelations and the Last Judgement. There are around 1,000 of these fantastic painted bosses throughout the cathedral. Use the computer in the south nave aisle to see each boss in detail, or view them in the wheeled looking glass, so you don't have to crane your neck.

The nave

The great copper font

The fonts

The great copper font is unique – it was a boiling pan from the Nestlé chocolate factory, given to the cathedral when the company left Norwich. A medieval stone font stands in St Luke's Chapel at the eastern end of the cathedral. This belonged to the lost church of St Mary-in-the-Marsh, which once stood inside the close.

Norwich Cathedral across the playing fields

The choir

Carved misericords, or tip-up 'mercy seats', where monks could rest during long services, are traditional within choir stalls. The carving on Norwich misericords is exceptional – and sometimes unexpected. Look closely among the medieval work for a modern depiction of former Norwich City Football Club goalkeeper Bryan Gunn. The splendid 14th-century pelican lectern, made of latten, a copper and zinc alloy, was buried for more than two centuries to escape destruction during the Reformation. The one-time belief that a pelican drew blood from its own breast to feed its young makes it a potent symbol of Christian belief.

Reaching heavenwards

The beautifully proportioned spire of Norwich Cathedral is, at 96 metres (315 feet), the second tallest in England after that of Salisbury. The present spire, atop the highest Norman tower in the country, was built in 1480, following three previous ones damaged by wind, fire and lightning.

The cathedral choir

The presbytery

This is the area before the high altar where you'll find the tomb of the cathedral's founder, Bishop Herbert de Losinga. On steps behind the altar is the bishop's wooden throne, or cathedra (from which we derive the word 'cathedral'), on top of the remains of an ancient stone Saxon throne.

Old bones

A gruesome skeleton carved on the wall of the south nave aisle is a memorial to one Thomas Gooding who was apparently buried standing up. A few lines of verse on the carving are a reminder of our own mortality.

Cathedral close

The cloisters

The size of the cathedral close, one of the largest in England, is a clue to its early days as a great monastic community where monks lived, travellers were given food, shelter and even medical treatment, and everyone came together to worship in the cathedral.

Upper Close

The west front of the cathedral looks onto a peaceful area of lawns, trees and seats. The buildings to the north of the Erpingham Gate are used by Norwich School, while the old Bishop's Palace (not open to visitors) is tucked away on the north side. On the south there is now a car park where once stood the infirmary, marked by the six 900-year-old pillars still standing. The grassy area to the east of the cathedral is the monks' burial ground, and here you'll also find the grave of Edith Cavell (see page 9).

West door

Flanking the cathedral's west door are two modern sculptures by David Holgate of writer and mystic Julian of Norwich (see page 15) and Saint Benedict, whose monastic rule was followed by the community of monks who lived here when the cathedral was founded.

Julian of Norwich   *Saint Benedict*

The Hostry

The Hostry took 11 years to complete and was part-funded by the Heritage Lottery Fund. Together with its sister building, the Refectory restaurant and coffee shop, it is the Cathedral's response to the needs of the new millennium. The Hostry Visitor & Education Centre is the main entrance to the Cathedral, where visitors enter through the original medieval arch used in the days of the priory. Its aim is to replicate the role of the original monastic Hostry, as a place where pilgrims and guests of Norwich Cathedral can be received in a Benedictine spirit of hospitality.

The cloisters

Cloisters were designed as walkways connecting different

Refectory

Hook's Walk

parts of the monastery and this is the largest monastic cloister in England. Look up to see the incredible carved and painted roof bosses,

including some very fine 'green men', and note the different styles of tracery (the patterns in the windows above the columns looking towards the enclosed lawn). Then look more closely at the lawn – it was turned into a labyrinth in 2002 to celebrate HM the Queen's Golden Jubilee.

Lower Close

A roadway from St Ethelbert Gate leads to the Lower Close where the houses are mainly residential. Hook's Walk, a picturesque path to the left, takes you to Bishopgate and the Great Hospital, founded in 1249 by Bishop Walter de Suffield as an almshouse for the needy and for 'poor and decrepit chaplains'. The building is now used for functions, concerts and charity events.

Prior's Door

13

King Street

Not far from Tombland, down quiet King Street, once lined by the houses of powerful Norwich merchants, stands magnificent Dragon Hall, unique in Europe. This building was the enormous trading hall of rich Norwich mercer, mayor and Member of Parliament, Robert Toppes. The only hall of its type to have survived in England, it was rediscovered in the 1970s and fully restored by 2006.

Dragon Hall

Interior of Dragon Hall

Dragon Hall

This lovely building's original existence was a short one. Built by Robert Toppes in about 1430 to dramatically display the goods that he imported by boat up the River Wensum from Europe, it was sold and split up on his death just 40 years later. Toppes, a member of the Guild of St George, used the dragon motif in his huge hall, with its oak-timbered roof. Just one beautifully carved dragon survives as a spandrel in these timbers, giving the hall its modern name. Toppes had his private staithe (landing stage) behind the hall to load the fine cloth he manufactured and exported, and unload the goods he then imported on the return journey. The front door opened onto King Street, the main road through 15th-century Norwich, then one of the most powerful towns in the whole of England. No wonder merchants came from all over to buy his goods.

Julian of Norwich's cell

St Ethelbert Gate

Here be dragons

The rich and powerful of Norwich belonged to the Guild of St George (founded in 1389) and the dragon theme continues in the city. In the great keep of the Castle Museum you'll see 'Snap', a focal point of the St George's Day procession, while the cathedral's St Ethelbert Gate is decorated with St George fighting a great dragon. In St Gregory's Church in Pottergate, wall paintings show St George and the dragon, and carved dragons are a feature of the dining hall of the Great Hospital at Bishopgate.

Julian of Norwich

'All shall be well and all shall be well and all manner of things shall be well,' wrote Julian of Norwich, mystic and anchoress, in her book Revelations of Divine Love. Julian lived in seclusion in a tiny room attached to the church that is named after her in St Julian's Alley. She was the first woman to write a book in the English language. It deals with her perception of divine love which she received in a series of visions in May 1373. The church and the nearby Julian Centre will help you discover more about this remarkable woman.

The Music House

Built in 1175 by a wealthy Jewish merchant, this is the oldest domestic house in the city. The building is now part of Wensum Lodge, an adult education centre.

The riverside

When you walk down the path that runs through the cathedral close from St Ethelbert Gate towards the river, you are following the line of a canal dug in the 11th century so that boats could bring imported stone for the cathedral from the River Wensum. The canal was filled in during the 18th century. You'll pass private houses and old stables, behind which are the

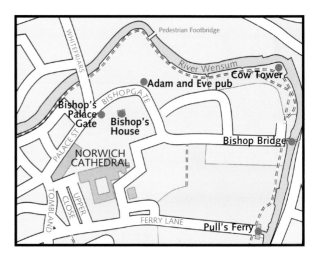

playing fields of Norwich School. A low archway, with the river beyond, marks the water gate, the point at which the river was channelled to form the canal.

Pull's Ferry

Pull's Ferry

It was on the riverbank through this archway that James Pull operated his rowing-boat ferry through the first half of the 19th century, until his death in 1841. A ferry continued to operate here for 100 more years, as a short cut across the river. Now people come to sit or walk by the water.

Bishop Bridge

The riverside walk takes you past Bishop Bridge, the oldest in Norwich, dating from 1340. A fortified gatehouse, part of the city defences, once stood beside the bridge.

The bricks on the parapet were added in the 1930s when the bridge received an eleventh-hour reprieve from demolition. Watercolour-artist John Cotman's view from this bridge, which you can see in the Castle Museum, shows warehouses and wherries (sailing barges) from when the river was alive with trading boats bringing goods in and out of Norwich.

Bishop Bridge

Cow Tower

Another part of Norwich's medieval fortifications, this brick and flint tower, built in 1378, inhabits a peaceful grassy part of the riverbank where for many years cows used to graze.

Adam and Eve pub

The path crosses a small footbridge. The inlet you are crossing was a swan pit in the grounds of the Great Hospital where birds were fattened for the table. Keep to the left-hand path, which takes you

to Bishopgate and the Dutch-gabled Adam and Eve pub, built where an inn has stood since the 13th century.

Adam and Eve pub

Bishop's Palace Gate

This 700-year-old entry into the cathedral close has two archways – one for walkers and a larger archway for carriages. Across the road is St Martin at Palace Plain where a grand three-storied Georgian house can be seen. This was the home of artist John Cotman. A short walk takes you back to Tombland and the cathedral.

Cow Tower

Elm Hill

Elm Hill, a quaint cobbled street opening out into a little square at whose heart is a large tree, epitomizes medieval Norwich. The tree is now a London plane rather than an elm, but the street itself is still pure 16th century. The street, with access to the river, was a residential area between the 16th and 18th centuries, and was where the wealthy of Norwich lived, in fine timber-framed houses.

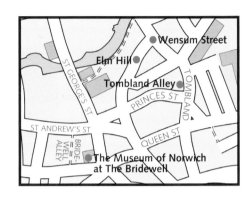

Plaque in Tombland Alley

Tombland Alley

Before walking down Wensum Street look into Tombland Alley, which connects Tombland with Princes Street and lies directly opposite the cathedral's Erpingham Gateway. Plague victims were buried here behind the high walls. The crooked timber-framed house by the entrance belonged to rich mercer Augustine Steward, mayor of Norwich three times during the mid-16th century. Look closely at the plaque on the wall to see a strange mark inscribed – each mercer had his own trading 'squiggle' that distinguished his goods from the others.

Wensum Street

This ancient street leads to 'Norwich over the Water', but before reaching the river turn left into Elm Hill. On the corner there's another of Norwich's ancient churches. Dedicated to St Simon and St Jude this tiny church, one of the oldest in the city, was saved from demolition by the Norwich Society – as was Elm Hill itself. There are monuments inside the deconsecrated church to the Pettus

Elm Hill

family, important citizens in the 16th and 17th centuries, whose house can be seen on Elm Hill.

Elm Hill

When the merchants moved out, many of the great houses were torn down, their gardens were built over and the street gradually became a slum. Things were so bad by the early 20th century that demolition of the area was mooted. Elm Hill was saved by the casting vote of the Lord Mayor at a council meeting in 1924, and the Norwich Society – which has done much to preserve many of the city's fine buildings – set to work. Look out for Pettus House, the

The Museum of Norwich at The Bridewell

Bridewell Alley

home of Sir John Pettus, who was knighted by Elizabeth I. Opposite, by Towler's Court, once the entrance to a shawl factory, is a path to the river.

The Museum of Norwich at The Bridewell

Walk down St Andrew's Street and turn up Bridewell Alley to the museum. Over the past 700 years the site has been home to powerful merchants, a house of correction, a factory and a museum. Now it tells the story of Norwich and its people, and benefits from a £1.5m refurbishment completed in 2012.

Norwich Lanes

Norwich is renowned for its old twisting streets full of enticing shops. You'll find many of them in the 'lanes' area, leading to peaceful St Giles and the Roman Catholic Cathedral Church of St John the Baptist.

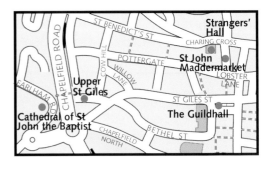

The Lanes

These narrow, often cobbled streets and alleys contain a variety of individual and unusual shops, cafés and small restaurants. Some have wonderfully evocative names – Upper Goat Lane, Lower Goat Lane, Labour in Vain Yard, Dove Street, Pottergate, Lobster Lane and St John Maddermarket; while some are more prosaic – Exchange Street, Bedford Street and London Street.

Strangers' Hall

Norwich Lanes Summer Fayre

Maddermarket Theatre

Maddermarket

As you walk along Lobster Lane you'll see St John Maddermarket on the right, where dyes for the cloth manufactured in the city were sold ('madder' is a plant from which a red dye was obtained). The theatre here takes its name from the ancient street. Nearby Charing Cross was once called 'Shearing' Cross because that was where the shearmen, who prepared the wool for the cloth, lived.

Strangers' Hall

The building which this beautifully laid out museum inhabits dates back nearly 700 years. It is open two days a week during the winter and four days from May to September. Each room shows a different historic period, while collections include toys and shop signs. The hall is possibly named for the religious refugees, known as 'strangers', from the Netherlands who settled here in the late 16th century.

Upper St Giles

Busy St Giles Street turns into the quiet shop-lined cul-de-sac of Upper St Giles Street. The church of St Giles on the Hill has an impressive tower, the tallest of the city's many churches, while the building is 14th century.

Cathedral of St John the Baptist

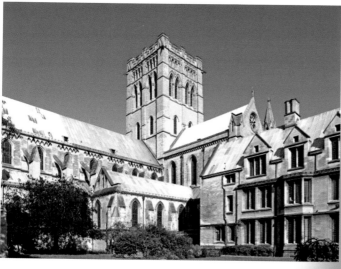

The Guildhall

You can't miss this outstanding early 15th-century building with its chequered wall. The offices of Norwich Heritage Economic and Regeneration Trust (HEART), the organisation behind the Norwich 12 initiative, are based here. Caley's cocoa café is also housed here.

The Guildhall

Cathedral of St John the Baptist

This imposing building is not as old as it looks (work started in 1894) but it is very fine with notable stained glass and black marble, polished to reveal thousands of fossils. It was designed by George Gilbert Scott junior and is a splendid example of Victorian Gothic revival.

One-time waterway

Lobster Lane, like many other lanes in Norwich, follows the line of a 'cockey' or a stream, where the water once ran down to the river.

Chapelfield

A shopping mall and a long-established formal garden bring many people to this area where once stood a college for priests. You can reach it either from the Cathedral Church of St John the Baptist – cross the footbridge and walk back along Upper St Giles Street to Cleveland Road, taking the alleyway to Chapelfield Gardens – or from The Forum.

Chapelfield Gardens

This area is named after medieval St Mary's Chapel and it is where English archers in the 16th century lined up shoulder-to-shoulder to train for battle. Chapelfield was designed as a public garden in 1880 and has a bandstand – where Glenn Miller and his band played in 1944 – a giant chessboard and children's play area.

intu Chapelfield shopping centre

The Canaries

The little yellow songbird became part of Norwich's heritage when weavers, fleeing religious persecution in the Netherlands, settled here, bringing with them their canaries. Norwich City Football Club, in their yellow and green strip, has claimed the bird as its mascot and nickname.

Theatre Royal

One of Norfolk's top performance venues, the Theatre Royal has undergone many incarnations since it was founded in 1758. A display in the foyer tells you about its varied history.

The Assembly House

This grand Georgian House was built for public gatherings in 1754 on the site of a much older building. Now it houses a restaurant and exhibition galleries, which are open to the public and can be hired for special events.

The Assembly House

Norwich over the Water

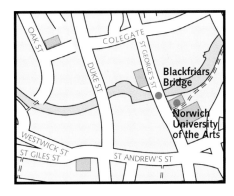

After the city walls were built in the late 13th century, the area north of the river, inhabited by wealthy merchants and once a flourishing trading centre, was known as Norwich over the Water. Today you'll find quiet streets full of well-preserved houses, cobbled lanes, many old churches and access to riverside walks.

Norwich University of the Arts

A mosaic in the entrance of the Norwich University of the Arts shows the Norwich arms, a castle and lion – and 20 bees, presumably signifying industriousness. The building was constructed in 1899 and above the doorway is another representation of the castle and lion. Across the road is the Norwich Gallery, belonging to the school, where you can see changing shows and exhibitions.

Blackfriars Bridge

Known as 'New Bridge' when it was built in the reign of Henry V, this river crossing is also called St George's Bridge after the street in which it stands. The present stone bridge was designed in 1794 by Bank of England architect Sir John Soane.

Norwich University of the Arts

Down by the river

There are many places in Norwich where you can join the quiet riverside walk, which runs for about 5 kilometres (3 miles) along the banks of the Wensum. Here you can join it at Blackfriars Bridge in St George's Street by Norwich University of the Arts, by Fye Bridge or at Elm Hill Quay.

Colegate

As you approach the Colegate area you'll see grand houses, set back from the quiet streets. The Harveys were a wealthy Norwich family in the 18th century and two of the grandest houses, Nos. 18 and 20, once belonged to them. The little church of St Clement's nearby contains many memorials to the Harveys.

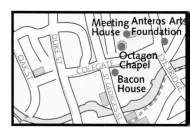

Octagon Chapel

Octagon Chapel

Thomas Ivory, who designed many of Norwich's grand 18th-century buildings, including the Assembly House and the original Theatre Royal (see page 22), conceived the idea of this grand Unitarian chapel, with wide carriage gates to allow entrance to the wealthy worshippers living in Colegate. It is built of brick with a grand portico, and eight magnificent decorated columns support the interior dome. Details of visiting times are on the door and you may use the little garden to the side.

Bacon House

This colour-washed half-timbered house, with its Norfolk flint base, on the corner of Colegate and St George's Street, was rebuilt in 1548 by rich cloth merchant Henry Bacon. It served time as a tobacco factory and a theatre but is now a private club.

Bacon House

The Old Meeting House

This simple red-brick place of worship was built for Norwich nonconformists in 1693 and has seen little change. It is used occasionally for services and is open to the public weekly. The sash windows in the red brick exterior are said to be the oldest in the city. The impressive interior is plain, with galleries on three sides overlooking rows of curving pews and a tall pulpit. Many marble memorials line the walls.

King of Hearts Café

King of Hearts Café

This unique café is set in a beautiful Tudor Merchant's House by the river and serves creative food from locally sourced ingredients.

Anteros Arts Foundation

In support of the visual arts, Anteros in Fye Bridge Street houses a gallery in a Tudor hall and also offers a venue for meetings, events and weddings. The Foundation also aims to develop practical creative skills by offering courses.

The Old Meeting House

Norfolk and the Norfolk Broads

The River Wensum, curling around the north and east of Norwich, was for many hundreds of years the city's main link with the outside world. Sea-going vessels and the sailing wherries that are still used for pleasure trips carried goods for the cloth-making and brewing businesses that brought prosperity to the city. Now the river is used mainly for leisure.

A wherry

The Broads

The Norfolk Broads, starting only two miles from the city, comprise 40 shallow lakes linked by rivers and are protected in the same way as a national park and looked after by the Broads Authority. These important wetlands, formed from medieval peat-diggings, are renowned as a wildlife habitat and an area where holidaymakers can enjoy boating, bird watching, fishing and walking.

The coast and inland

Long sandy beaches and traditional seaside resorts such as Cromer, Wells-next-the-Sea and Sheringham are good for family holidays, while grand houses such as Holkham Hall, Felbrigg Hall, Blickling Hall, Houghton Hall, Sandringham and Oxburgh Hall offer history and heritage.

Whitlingham Broad

Sign of greatness

All over Norfolk are carved signs peculiar to a particular town or village. Many were the work of Norfolk schoolmaster Harry Carter who started the practice in Swaffham in 1929. The sign in the market town of Hingham shows 17th-century parishioners embarking on the long journey to the Americas. One was Samuel Lincoln, whose direct descendant Abraham did pretty well for himself – he became President of the United States. A bust of the great man sits in the church of St Andrew's, Hingham.

Information

What's on
Full and up-to-date information on all events can be found at the Tourist Information Centre (see page 28).

January
Pantomime, Theatre Royal

Spring and Autumn
UEA Literary Festival

May
Norfolk and Norwich Festival;
The Broads Outdoors Festival
Norwich Film Festival

May/June
Norwich City of Ale

June
Royal Norfolk Show

July
Lord Mayor's Celebrations
Shakespeare Festival in
Norwich Cathedral cloisters
Norwich Lanes Summer Fayre

September
Heritage Open Days

October
Norwich Beer Festival;
Norwich Fringe Festival;
Norfolk Food & Drink Festival

November
Sparks in the Park (fireworks);
Christmas Lights

December
Norwich Christmas
Celebrations

Christmas Lights;
Pantomime, Theatre Royal

Tours and trips
Information on the following tours, and many others, can be found at the Tourist Information Centre, or on www.visitnorwich.co.uk.

Qualified guides lead a variety of walks from The Forum and the cathedral's Erpingham Gate. Tours of buildings and themed walks are also available.

City Boats operate trips and special cruises from Elm Hill Quay, Griffin Lane Quay and Station Quay.

Museums and galleries
Anteros Arts Foundation
01603 766129
www.anteros.co.uk

Assembly House
01603 626402, www.assembly
housenorwich.co.uk;
The Museum of Norwich at the Bridewell
01603 629127,
www.museums.norfolk.gov.uk;
Dragon Hall
01603 663922,
www.dragonhall.org;
King of Hearts Café
01603 620805,
www.kingofheartscafe.co.uk;
Norwich Arts Centre
01603 660352,
www.norwichartscentre.co.uk;
Norwich Castle Museum and Art Gallery
01603 493625,
www.museums.norfolk.gov.uk;
Sainsbury Centre for Visual Arts
01603 593199,
www.scva.org.uk;
Strangers' Hall
01603 667229,
www.museums.norfolk.gov.uk.

Sainsbury Centre for Visual Arts
This collection of works of art is housed in architect Norman Foster's first major public building, opened in 1978 at the University of East Anglia, on the outskirts of Norwich. In addition to the large permanent collections there are regular temporary exhibitions.

Front cover: Norwich Cathedral
with Wellington statue
Back cover: River Wensum

Acknowledgements
Photography by Neil Jinkerson
© Jarrold Publishing. Additional
photography by kind permis-
sion of: Alamy 27 (Jason Bye),
BC (David Moore); Norwich
Castle Museum 6cr; Norwich
Cathedral 10tl & r, 11t; Fisheye
Images 19br; Melanie March 20l;
© Paul Hurst 21t.

The publishers would like to
thank the staff of VisitNorwich,
Norwich Museums, Norwich
Cathedral and Blue Badge guide
Gwen Digby for their assistance
in the preparation of this guide.

Written by Annie Bullen; the
author has asserted her moral
rights.
Edited by Angela Royston.
Designed by Simon Borrough.
Additional picture research by
Jan Kean.
City map/park and ride map
by The Map Studio, Romsey,
Hants, UK; walk maps by Simon
Borrough; maps based on car-
tography © George Philip Ltd.

All information correct at time
of going to press, but may be
subject to change.

Printed in Great Britain.
ISBN 978-1-84165-560-4   1/14

i Tourist Information Centre (TIC)
The Forum,
Millennium Plain,
Norwich NR2 1TF
tel: 01603 213999
email: tourism@norwich.
gov.uk
website: www.visitnorwich.
co.uk.

Shopmobility
For the loan of manual
or electric wheelchairs and
powered scooters to those
who need them. Level 1,
intu Chapelfield Car Park
To book, tel: 01603 753350
Level 2, Castle Mall
To book, tel: 01603 283148

PITKIN CITY GUIDES

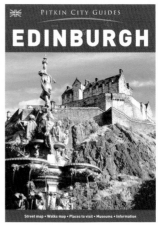

This guide is just one in a series of city titles